IMAGES OF ENGLAND

AROUND
ROTHWELL
VOLUME II

IMAGES OF ENGLAND

AROUND ROTHWELL
VOLUME II

SIMON BULMER AND ERIC WRIGHT

TEMPUS

This book is dedicated to the memory of
Colin William Bulmer
(1936 – 2002)
and
Frederick Charles Wright
(1903 – 1972)

First published 2004

Tempus Publishing Limited
The Mill, Brimscombe Port,
Stroud, Gloucestershire, GL5 2QG
www.tempus-publishing.com

British Library Cataloguing in Publication Data.
A catalogue record for this book is available from the British Library.

ISBN 0 7524 3365 2

Typesetting and origination by Tempus Publishing Limited.
Printed in Great Britain.

Contents

Acknowledgements

Simon and Eric would like to thank the following: Leeds City Council, Rothwell Library, Albert Brown, June Evans, Richard Evans, Heather Evens, Stephen Ward, Enid Bulmer, Members of Rothwell & District Historical Society, Mr Plumb, Mark Bennett, Audrey and David Rains, Terry Barton, Charles Brears, Brian Wright, Fr Paul Cressall, Doris Cassell, The Fox family, Pete and Wendy Ellis, Holy Trinity Parochial Council, Eileen Roberts, Rothwell Temperance Band, Joan Elliott, Yorkshire Fittings Ltd, Mrs Hardwick, Mrs V. Ward, Cllr Don Wilson, Sally Boulton, Haigh Road Infants School and to all those whose photographs are in this book but were not identifiable as the owners. Special thanks go to John Wright, Diane Moutrey and staff of Rothwell Library. Our sincere thanks go to Michelle Page for her valued help and assistance with this publication and to her dedication to local history. Finally we thank Susan, Charlotte, Emily and Margaret, who have put up with our constant disappearances while preparing this book.

Introduction

We are deeply proud to walk in the footsteps of an earlier generation of local historians such as John Batty, E.R. Manley, Jim Hardwick and William Hartley Banks and to have worked alongside Albert Brown and Harry Blowers who, to this day, are guardians over those earlier generations' knowledge. In our own way we have all strived to preserve and record the rich history that has made Rothwell the town it is today.

The first book *Around Rothwell (1999)* was a runaway success. It has helped the local community celebrate its heritage, and has gone on to be used as a reference book for academics in their research and in schools, colleges and universities. We recall, beaming with pride, that someone, somewhere, would be opening a Christmas present to find a book called *Around Rothwell* and saying to a grandchild, son or daughter 'I remember that!'

For all those would be authors out there I would like to share a thought. I was one of the first pupils to go to the now ill-fated Langdale Primary School in Woodlesford, way back in the early 1970s. I had very poor eyesight and was made to stand next to one particular teacher who remained seated. She asked me to read from the book on the table. I could not read a word! The teacher became increasingly agitated and in an irritable voice said that I could not read and would never be able to read. That comment stuck to me like glue for the rest of my school days. I was convinced that I could not read a book and didn't until I left secondary school. Guess what? She was wrong! So if you have a story to tell, go on, have a go and write it down.

Why *Around Rothwell, Volume II* you may ask yourself? Well, the truth is that there is still a wealth of photographs out there waiting to be shared with the local community and beyond, some that have been hidden from view for years. It helps promote the town and its history in countries throughout the world. Many people over the years have emigrated from the town to America, Canada, Africa, Australia and New Zealand and their families, who are aware of their history, are keen to look at the way their forebears lived. Again it is sharing with the wider, educational community, and helping the children of today learn about their town's past whilst trying to encourage them to preserve their history for generations to come.

The Rothwell Castle Project and The Rothwell Jack Project are at the forefront of the town's celebration of its rich heritage. Eric, the membership of Rothwell and District Historical Society and myself are proud to be associated with these great projects. This has been made possible by working in close partnership with other organisations such as Education Leeds, WYAS, Leeds City Council, English Heritage, Rothwell Parochial Council, Royal Armouries and Lord Mowbray. Both will help the community to understand the early history of the town by letting us read about life in Medieval and Tudor times, learn why the kings of England came to hunt in Rothwell Hunting Park and understand why the mighty John of Gaunt was supposed to have killed the last wild boar. These projects are where local folklore becomes fact and where we can celebrate the rich tapestry of the town's life from the early Anglo-Scandinavians to the Tudors.

As London has, over the years, assimilated its outlying villages and towns into one big metropolis, it is inevitable that as Leeds spreads its wings ever further we will see the merging of nearby towns and villages to create a Leeds metropolis. Individual towns and villages may loose their identity; therefore it has become a necessity to publish whatever we can to help future generations appreciate what was once there.

If this publication stirs a memory or two, or if you can tell someone a story about one of the photographs, then we will have done our jobs well.

Simon Bulmer & Eric Wright
June 2004

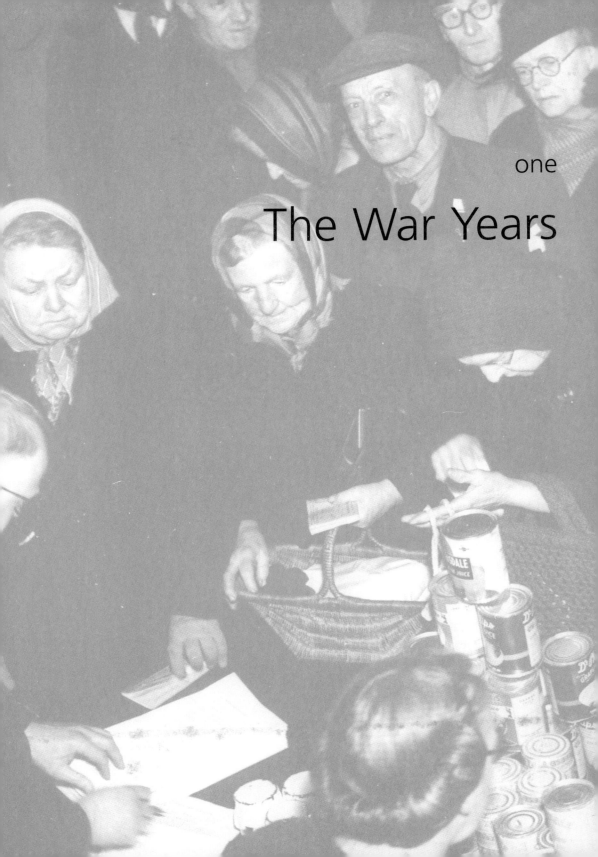

one

The War Years

This picture, taken in 1944, shows a RUDC mobile canteen. which was one of a small fleet of vans in Rothwell during the war.

Four mobile canteen vans supplied by YMCA and WVS with RUDC civic dignitaries outside Rothwell Council Offices in 1944.

RUDC employees enjoy a cup of tea from one of the mobile canteens during the Second World War.

The presentation of a souvenir lighter to the armed forces by the chairman of the RUDC, W.E. Moorhouse and Hon. Sec. R. Nicholson to Able Seaman Robinson, Driver Moore, Pte J. Wilson and Flg-Off Hoult, late 1940s.

Above and below: This picture taken in the 1940s is of the seventh distribution of food gifts to the over-seventy-year-olds, which proved very timely for Christmas. Much appreciation was voiced by the pensioners at the eight distribution centres in the RUDC area. Councillors of each ward shared in the distribution of nearly 5,000 packages of food. Sides of bacon had been sliced by local trades people and made into ½ lbs packs and fat had been rendered down by the butchers and put into 1lb cartons. Jam, tinned steak, mincemeat, malted, evaporated and condensed milk, flour, apricots, peas, butter, margarine, marmalade, fruit juices, tea, chocolate, corn beef, dried eggs, tongue and suet also figured in the gifts, of which each aged person was given three packages.

ROTHWELL URBAN DISTRICT COUNCIL.

Extensions to Council Offices

OFFICIAL OPENING
WEDNESDAY, MARCH 27th, 1940, 6.0 p.m.

The pleasure of the company of

....

is requested on the above occasion.

Tea at 5.0 p.m. at the Council Offices, Rothwell.

The Council Chamber and Offices will be open for inspection
between the hours of 4.30 to 6.0 p.m.

The official invitation to the opening of the RUDC council office extension on 27 March 1940.

A group photograph showing invited guests at the official opening of the new council offices extension in 1940.

A picture of the completed council offices extension just prior to its opening.

Opposite above: This photograph was taken in Rothwell Park during Merchant Navy Week of autumn 1945 and shows the crowning of the Merchant Navy Queen. From left to right, back row are: J.C. Harrison, Mrs Smart, Cllr Smart, C. Overbury, E.F. Moorhouse, Mrs Dobson, W.E. Moorhouse, Mrs Capewell. Front row: Cllr Blackman, Cllr Capewell, Miss Oaks, Miss Cheeseborough, Miss Benford (Queen), Miss Butterfield and Miss Davies.

Opposite below left: An official photograph of Cllr Armitage, the chairman of the RDUC from 1940 to '41, who was also a joiner and undertaker in Stourton.

Opposite below right: An official photograph of Cllr G. Simpson, the chairman of the RUDC from 1943 to '44.

Rothwell Army volunteers' group photograph, taken in 1914.

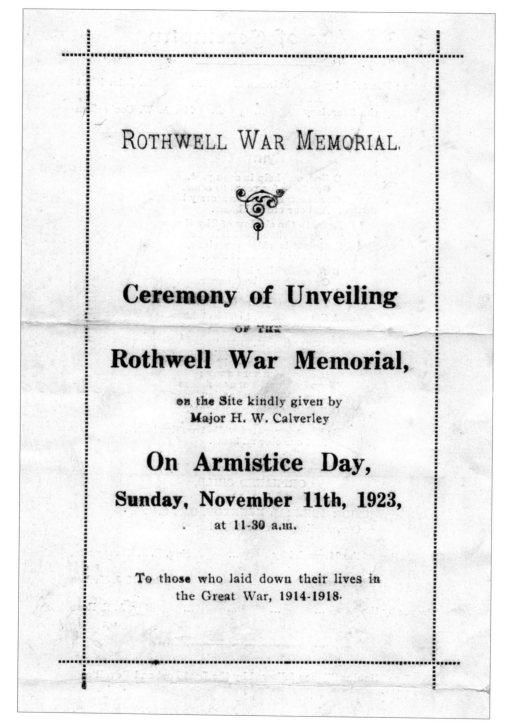

ROTHWELL WAR MEMORIAL.

Ceremony of Unveiling

OF THE

Rothwell War Memorial,

on the Site kindly given by
Major H. W. Calverley

On Armistice Day,

Sunday, November 11th, 1923,

at 11-30 a.m.

To those who laid down their lives in
the Great War, 1914-1918.

This brochure was published for the unveiling of Rothwell war memorial on Sunday
11 November 1923. Maj. H.W. Calverley donated the land to Rothwell for this memorial.

A picture of the newly unveiled Rothwell war memorial, 1923.

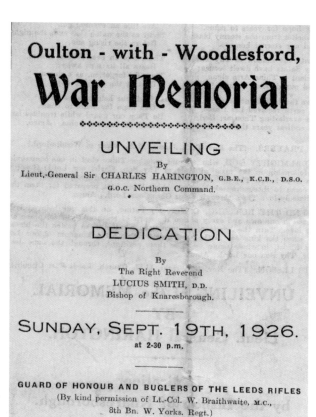

Oulton - with - Woodlesford,
War Memorial

❖❖❖❖❖❖❖❖❖❖❖❖❖❖❖❖❖❖❖❖❖❖❖❖❖❖❖

UNVEILING

By
Lieut.-General Sir CHARLES HARINGTON, G.B.E., K.C.B., D.S.O.
G.O.C. Northern Command.

DEDICATION

By
The Right Reverend
LUCIUS SMITH, D.D.
Bishop of Knaresborough.

SUNDAY, SEPT. 19TH, 1926.

at 2-30 p.m.

GUARD OF HONOUR AND BUGLERS OF THE LEEDS RIFLES
(By kind permission of Lt.-Col. W. Braithwaite, M.C.,
8th Bn. W. Yorks. Regt.)

This brochure was published to commemorate the unveiling of Oulton with Woodlesford war memorial, on Sunday 19 September 1926. It was unveiled by Lt-Gen Sir Charles Harrington and dedicated by Lucius Smith the Bishop of Knaresborough. The buglers of the Leeds Rifles provided a guard of honour and Oulton Band accompanied the hymns.

The Oulton with Woodlesford war memorial in the 1920s.

Robin Hood war memorial at the junction of Sharpe Lane and Wakefield Road in the 1920s.

Here Cllr E. Horner opens Warship Week in 1942. £142,215 was raised during Rothwell's Warship Week and this more than doubled their target of £70,000 for Motor Torpedo Boat 235. Village totals were Methley £28,033, Stourton £12,660, Oulton £10,117, Woodlesford £9,989, Carlton £11,528, Robin Hood and Rothwell Haigh £10,310, Lofthouse £10,443, Thorpe £6,608 and Rothwell £42,725, no mean feat during the lean war years.

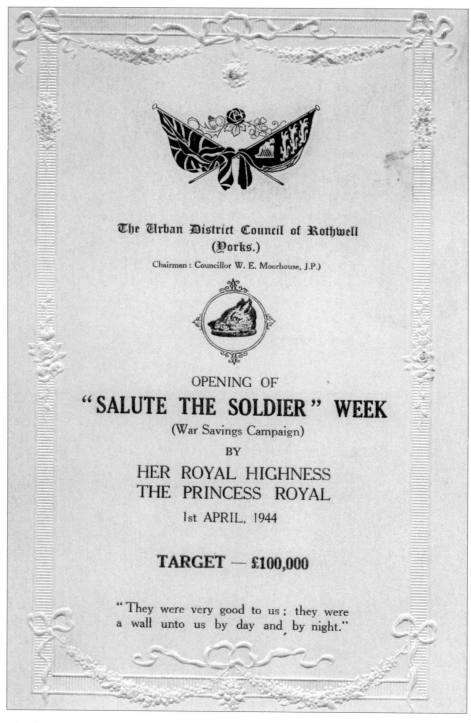

The Urban District Council of Rothwell
(Yorks.)

Chairman : Councillor W. E. Moorhouse, J.P.)

OPENING OF

"SALUTE THE SOLDIER" WEEK

(War Savings Campaign)

BY

HER ROYAL HIGHNESS
THE PRINCESS ROYAL

1st APRIL, 1944

TARGET — £100,000

"They were very good to us ; they were
a wall unto us by day and by night."

This brochure celebrated Salute the Soldier week, which began on 1 April 1944. HRH Princess Royal attended the Rothwell celebrations.

This line up of dignitaries was taken during the celebrations of Salute the Soldier week in April 1944. From left to right are: Maj. Morris, Hon. Gerald Lascelles, P.H. Briggs, Dr W. Hargreaves, Cllr E. Horner and Ald. Sir William Cartright.

Air Raid Wardens on parade on Marsh Street during the celebrations for Salute the Soldier week in April 1944.

HRH Princess Royal addressing the crowd in Marsh Street in April 1944, as part of the celebrations of Salute the Soldier week.

This photograph of HRH Princess Royal was taken outside the council offices in April 1944 as part of the celebration for Salute the Soldier week. Pictured are Cllr E. Horner, T.J. Brooks MP, E.F. Moorhouse, Lt–Col. Longden, Miss Beryl Green (school child), P.R. Farrer and Cllr W. Hoult in April 1944.

Local Boy Scouts on parade on Marsh Street during the celebration for Salute the Soldier week in April 1944.

HRH Princess Royal visiting Yorkshire Copper Works. From left to right are: HRH Princess Royal, J.A. Sykes, H.F. Sherborne and E. Duffield. This was part of Salute the Soldier week.

A group of students from Rothwell Grammar School before they set off for a trip to France in May 1939. This would only have been four months before the outbreak of the Second World War and Hitler's plans to invade Poland were well advanced.

RUDC councillors in 1938-39. From left to right, back row: Cllrs Smart, Armitage, Philips, Simpson, Edwards, Wilson and Cockayne. Middle row: Cllrs Roberts, Tasker, Jones, Holman, Chilton, Moorhouse, Jackson, Caygill, Horner and Holroyd. Front row: Cllrs Slater, Blackburn, Moorhouse, Newsome, Killingbeck, Hoult, Wilkinson and Hollings.

two

Yorkshire
Copper Works

This picture, taken during the First World War, shows how important the role of the woman was during the war years.

This gentleman is Jack Higgins who, during the Depression of the late 1920s and early 1930s, was out of work for a number of years. He is shown here in his best suit, ready to walk into Leeds to collect the entertainment's licence for Rothwell Mechanics Institute. While he was walking past the Yorkshire Copper Works he saw a queue of men waiting for work and thought he should join it. As the manager came along the line he was picked and had to dig ditches all day in his best suit. His career at the Yorkshire Copper Works lasted forty-seven years.

An aerial view of the Yorkshire Copper Works site in 1962.

Staff spend their spare time looking at a Typhoon aircraft that formed part of a wartime exhibition, which was held on the Yorkshire Copper Works site in the later war years.

Servicemen pictured with the directors of the Yorkshire Copper Works posing in front of a Typhoon aircraft during the Second World War.

Staff at the Yorkshire Copper Works enjoy an exhibition during the Second World War .

Adm. Sir Edward Evans visits to Yorkshire Copper Works site on 31 August 1940.

A scene from an exhibition held at Yorkshire Copper Works site during 1939.

Another exhibition at the Yorkshire Copper Works in October 1931 showing the Leeds Model and Engineering Society's exhibition stand.

ONE SET OF OIL PIPES FOR TURRET.

ROSE.MK.I. ·5 TURRET.
AS FITTED IN LANCASTERS.
DESIGNED AND MANUFACTURED BY
ROSE BROS (GAINSBOROUGH) LTD ·,
ALBION WORKS,
GAINSBOROUGH. LINCS.

THIS TURRET HAS COMPLETED
MORE THAN 100 OPERATIONS
OVER ENEMY TERRITORY.

A Rose MK.1 Turret, was exhibited at the Yorkshire Copper works in 1939

The Yorkshire Copper Works, photographed in 1938, showing the completed of No. 9 mill.

Mill No. 5 at Yorkshire Copper Works in 1931.

Haigh Park Road Stourton looking towards the Yorkshire Copper Works in April 1934.

A bus strike in 1957 meant that the staff of the Yorkshire Copper Works had to resort to using the newly acquired ERF open lorries to get home after their shifts. At least one of the buses belonged to local owner Clifford Lunn.

Work begins on the construction of mill No. 9 at the Yorkshire Copper Works site in 1937.

Another view of the later stages of construction of mill No.9 in 1937.

External view of the construction of mill No. 9 in 1937.

This shows the completed construction of mill No. 9 and the installation of machinery in 1937–38.

Above left: The arrival, by rail, of the first parts of a 3,000/3,500 horizontal press to the Yorkshire Copper Works in 1937.

Above right: The beginning of work to connect a furnace at the Yorkshire Copper Works in 1937.

Right: Another view of the internal machinery of mill No. 9 in 1937.

Further work being completed on machinery in mill No. 9 in 1937.

Another view of the work being carried out on machinery in mill No. 9 in 1937.

This picture shows the main ram, weighing in at 36 tons, being pulled clear of the railway wagon. The work had to be carried out by the use of jacks and winches and it was finally moved 60 yards to its installation site.

The arrival of the main cylinder of the 3,000/3,500 horizontal press weighing in at 42 tons, in 1937.

The marquees are in readiness for children's day, a popular event in the 1940s and 1950s at the Yorkshire Copper Works.

One of the newly acquired ERF open lorries used by the Yorkshire Copper Works in the 1950s, shown here in a snow storm next to the Coronation Garden.

three

Mining and Quarrying

This is the winder, Wilfred Haigh, in winding house No.1 at Water Haigh Colliery in Woodlesford in 1968. The leaver on the left is the forward reverse and the centre lever is for steam power. The right leaver operated the governed speed the cage would travel down the shaft, one way bringing 'coal up' the other way 'men riding'.

Right: Water Haigh Colliery in Woodlesford in 1968. Here workers are pouring hot lead into the rope capple.

Below: A photograph taken in 1968 of men at Water Haigh Colliery holding the end of the No. 3 winding rope while the binding rings are hammered tightly down, so as to grip the rope and hold the capple in place. This was then fitted on to the lifting gear and cage.

An NCB steam locomotive in the yard of Water Haigh Colliery in the 1960s. The Armitages railway was also used by the stone quarry and the brickworks.

The NCB locomotive working near to Woodlesford brickworks in the 1960s.

An NCB locomotive passes under the Midland main line located down Fleet Lane at Oulton in the 1960s.

A locomotive takes a side line to were the coal waste was tipped just off Fleet Lane in Woodlesford in the 1960s.

J. & J. CHARLESWORTH LIMITED.

FANNY COLLIERY.

◆

PITHEAD BATHS.

◆

The tablet bears the following inscription :

MINERS' WELFARE FUND.

FANNY COLLIERY PITHEAD BATHS.

◆

THESE BATHS, ERECTED BY THE MINERS' WELFARE COMMITTEE IN PURSUANCE OF THE MINING INDUSTRY ACT 1926, WERE OPENED BY

MRS. A. K. CHARLESWORTH,

AND HANDED OVER TO THE TRUSTEES ON THE 9TH. JUNE. 1934.

AFTER THE OPENING CEREMONY.

NOTE :– After the Opening Ceremony, those present will have an opportunity of going through the bath house. On Sunday, the 10th. June, 1934, the bath house will be open from 10 a.m. to 8 p.m, for anyone who wishes to bring his relations to see it.

J. W. V. Parminter & Son Limited, Printers, 18, King Street, Wakefield.

This brochure celebrates the opening ceremony of the Fanny Pit baths on 9 June 1934 by Mrs A.K. Charlesworth, the wife of one of the colliery owners.

VIEW FROM THE SOUTH OF
FANNY COLLIERY AND PITHEAD BATHS

A view of the newly built Fanny Pit baths in June 1934.

One of the last photographs taken of miners from the doomed Fanny Pit in the early 1980s.

This former building at the Low Shops Colliery was all that remained of the Boulton and Watt engine installed in the 1700s when it was photographed here in the 1960s.

The last remains of the horse gin were still in position in the 1960s at Low Shops Colliery. It was later removed to Halifax museum.

Right: This view shows the new engine house at Low Shops in the early 1900s.

Below: This picture of Rose pit also shows the remains of Rothwell Castle. It is worth noting the size of the castle stump at this time as compared to its much reduced appearance today.

ROTHWELL HAIGH COLLIERY, SHEWING OLDCASTLE, 1447.

This view of Rose pit was taken in the 1960s from the top of Rothwell parish church and clearly shows the extent of its workings and waste. They later spread right across the pastures.

This is the pit yard of Water Haigh Colliery at Woodlesford, during the 1970s.

This view of Water Haigh Colliery at Woodlesford was taken from Fleet lane in the 1970s.

Above: These pictures show what remained of the buildings at Taty Main Colliery in Carlton by the 1970s. This colliery was a drift mine with underground connections to a number of other pits.

Above left: The remains of the winding gear at Robin Hood Colliery in the 1970s.

Above right: Arnold's sand quarry at the end of John O'Gaunts Walk in the 1930s.

Thorpe quarry photographed in the 1950s, clearly showing the alternating layers of rock and shale.

In a distant time the parish of Rothwell formed part of a vast tropical swamp where bamboos and giant ferns grew in abundance. Some of them were preserved as fossils in the swamp mud, which eventually turned into shale. These specimens were found in the shale at Thorpe Quarry in 1959.

Ripples made by the sea on the seashore millions of years ago have been preserved in this bed of sandstone discovered in 1954. The sand was overlaid by tons of shale and other deposits, which resulted in its compression into stone.

A general view of George Armitage's Brickworks at Thorpe showing exposed coal seams.

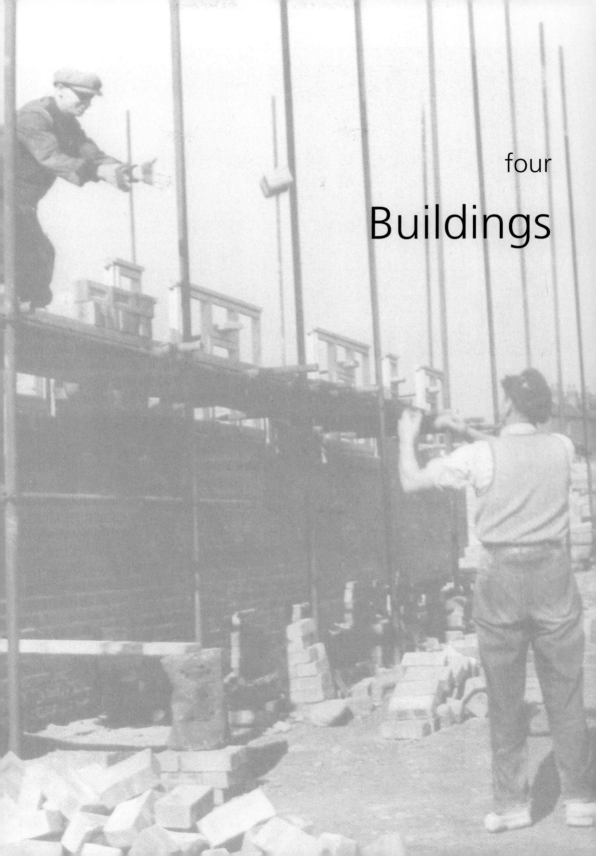

four

Buildings

Rothwell Urban District.

NEW COUNCIL OFFICES.

T. H. & W. E. RICHARDSON,

ARCHITECTS,

28, BOND ST., LEEDS,
JUNE 8TH, 1895.

LEEDS & ROTHWELL.

This brochure was produced in 1895 by T.H. Richardson and W.E. Richardson, who were to build the new council offices.

A view of the Black Bull public house in Commercial Street Rothwell.

This sad picture of Rothwell Manor House was taken during the late 1970s, prior to its demolition in 1977.

This house which was just off Westgate Lane in Lofthouse was once a school. It is seen here in the 1950s.

The RUDC glasshouses at the bottom end of Rothwell Park near to Gillett lane seen during winter floods in the 1970s.

Remains of Rothwell Castle in the 1950s with Barrett's Mill in the background.

The interior of Carlton Rope Works in the 1950s.

Skeins of twine produced at Carlton Rope Works in the 1950s.

The Mechanics Institute on Marsh Street, Rothwell in the 1950s.

The water wheel, that drove the machinery in Barrett's mill seen here in the 1950s.

This 1930s-style house, which was located on Leeds Road, has since be demolished to make way for a more modern development.

The weir at Fleet Mill on the river Aire in the 1950s, when there was still a village of Fleet.

One of the water wheels at Fleet Mills, destroyed in a fire in the 1920s.

This area once formed part of a pinfold in Carlton and was used, in the days of common grazing land, for impounding animals that belonged to people who did not possess grazing rights or whose cattle strayed. It was photographed here in the 1950s

Construction of the lower school of Royds started in the 1950s.

A postcard picture of Rothwell Secondary Modern School, now Royds High School. This view shows what was a later addition to the lower school built in the 1950s.

Some of the first buildings on Quarry Hill in Oulton of the housing development that was complete by the late 1950s.

A scene at the junction of Holmsley Field Lane in Oulton, showing Harold Hall prior to the development of the late 1950s.

The early stages of construction of the Wood Lane Estate in 1952.

Foundations being laid for houses on the new Wood Lane Estate in 1952.

Bricklaying starts on new houses on the Wood Lane Estate.

Finally the roofs go on at the Wood Lane Estate.

New houses go up in Ouzlewell Green, late 1950s.

Opposite above: Fish Hole Yard in Carlton.

Opposite below: John Waddington's works at Stourton, 1986. The firm was known worldwide for its board games.

ROTHWELL URBAN DISTRICT COUNCIL

SOUVENIR
OF THE NEW
SEWAGE
DISPOSAL
WORKS

Opened by

WILLIAM LUNN, M.P.

SEPTEMBER 10th, 1930

This souvenir brochure was published to celebrate the opening of the RUDC sewage works at Oulton on 10 September 1930.

ROTHWELL SEWAGE DISPOSAL WORKS.

NEERS:
MESSRS. WILLCOX & RAIKES, MM. Inst. C.E.
BIRMINGHAM.

CONTRACTORS:
THE PROVINCIAL CONSTRUCTION
SUNDERLAND.

An aerial view of the new RUDC sewage disposal works at Lemon Royd in Fleet Lane, Oulton 1930.

Settling tanks and bacteria beds at Lemon Royd sewage disposal works, 1930.

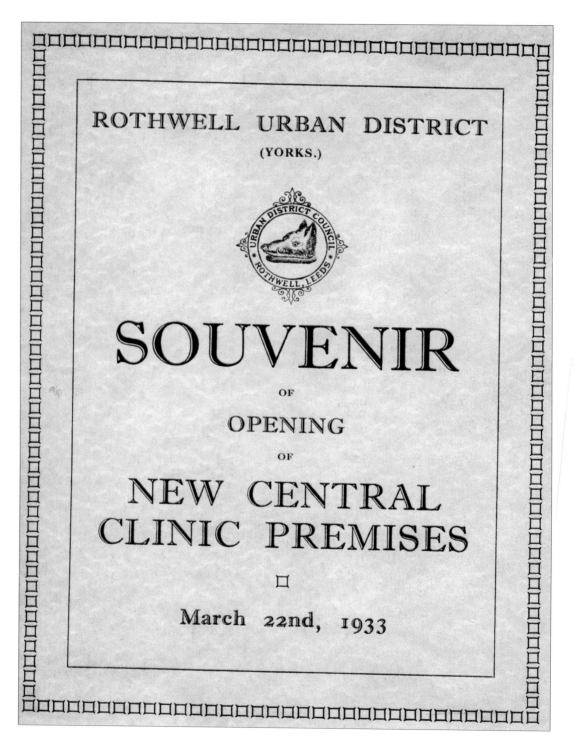

ROTHWELL URBAN DISTRICT
(YORKS.)

SOUVENIR

OF

OPENING

OF

NEW CENTRAL
CLINIC PREMISES

□

March 22nd, 1933

This souvenir brochure was published to celebrate the opening of the RUDC Central Clinic in Oulton Lane on 22 March 1933.

Invited guests at the opening of the RUDC Central Clinic 1933. Not all the names are known but among those in the back row are: Jackson, Snell, Lunn, Wade, Hartley, Dobson, Chapman. Middle row: Harvey, Chambers, Stevenson, Brown, Moorhouse, Robinson, Blackburn, Lawrence, Turner and Abram. Front row: Cameron, Turnbull, Oaks and Cook.

A picture of the RUDC Central Clinic in Oulton Lane in 1935.

A view of the shop premises belonging to Annie Wilkinson who lived at No. 1 Fearnside Fold at Lofthouse. The photograph is thought to have been taken sometime in the 1920s.

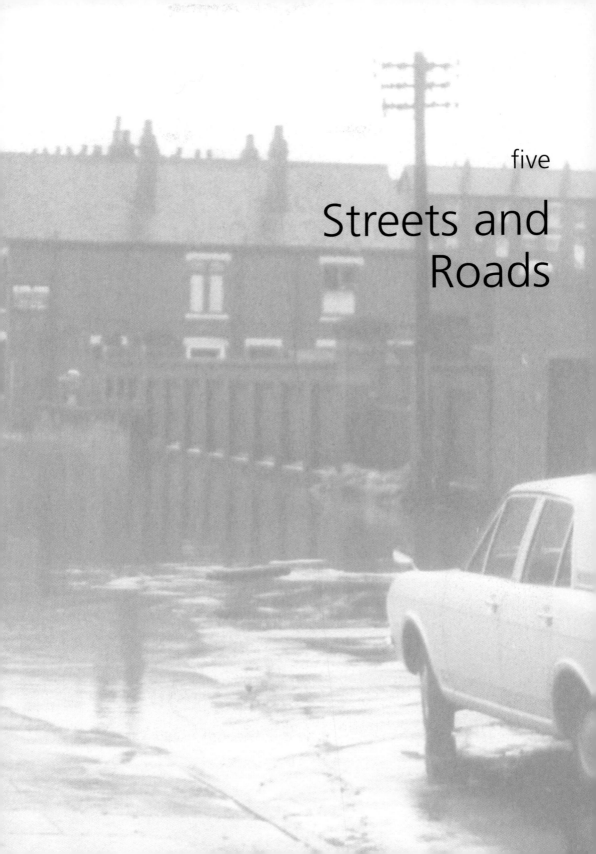

five

Streets and
Roads

A crack caused by subsidence appeared on Bell Hill in Rothwell during September 1935.

A view of the junction of Woodlesford Lane and Styebank Lane, *c.* 1920.

Children playing in snow in Royds Lane in the early 1900s.

This is a view of Cross Street, Rothwell in 1935. Note the lack of proper pavements or surfaced road.

Commercial Street Tram Terminus outside the Black Bull in the 1920s.

Wood Lane, looking over the pastures to the home of Garnett Higgins, a local character and former postman for the village photographed in the1970s.

This row of terraced houses was located just off Carlton Lane near the fire station.

A Rolls Royce makes its way between snow drifts on Longthorpe Lane near to Rodillian School in 1937 .

This picture was taken from Holmsley Field Lane, Oulton. It shows a field that had been used in the 1960s and '70s for grazing livestock. Originally a metal fence separated the playground of Oulton Primary School, the remains of which can be seen in the distance, and the farmer's field. A favoured playing area for local children was the air-raid shelter of Oulton School playground.

Children and passers-by pose for a photograph in Wakefield Road in Rothwell Haigh outside the Angel pub in around 1910.

Wagons Yard just off Marsh Street.

A flood at the bottom of Carlton Lane was photographed in the 1970s.

Flooding by the parish church and the White Swan pub in the 1970s.

Flood waters spread up Meynell Avenue, 1970s.

A cold, snowy scene in Commercial Street by the Coach and Horses pub.

This picture shows the narrowing of Meynell Avenue, which leads into Churchfield Lane, later widened to accommodate modern traffic.

This building still remains at the junction of Sharpe Lane and Wakefield Road in Robin Hood. It was originally a repeater station used by the RAF.

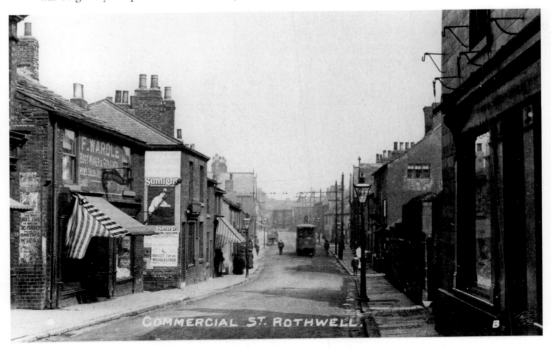

This photograph shows the end of Commercial Street. Note F. Wardle, boot-maker and repairer's shop on the left and the rare view of a single decker tram in Rothwell.

Opposite above: The stationmaster's house at Woodlesford at the junction of Station Lane and Aberford Road in the early 1900s.

Opposite below: The Co-op building on Aberford Road in Woodlesford, early 1900s.

Left: An early view of Church Street in Woodlesford in the early 1900s.

Below: The top end of Church Street, Woodlesford early 1900s.

CHURCH ST. WOODLESFORD.

ABERFORD RP. WOODLESFORD.

This picture was taken from Leeds Road, Lofthouse and shows Ledger Lane's Co-op shop in the 1950s.

This Ineson postcard photograph of Methley was taken in around 1904.

A view of Farrar Lane, Oulton near where the Dolphin River runs under the road and near to what used to be Knowles Farm.

The Three Horse Shoes pub looking down St Johns Street towards Vine Cottage.

Queen Elizabeth II's Silver Jubilee celebrations in 1977 in East View, Oulton. The children enjoy food and drink at trestle tables set up in the street. Alice Topping and Jack Higgins, standing on the left, look on as the children enjoy the celebrations.

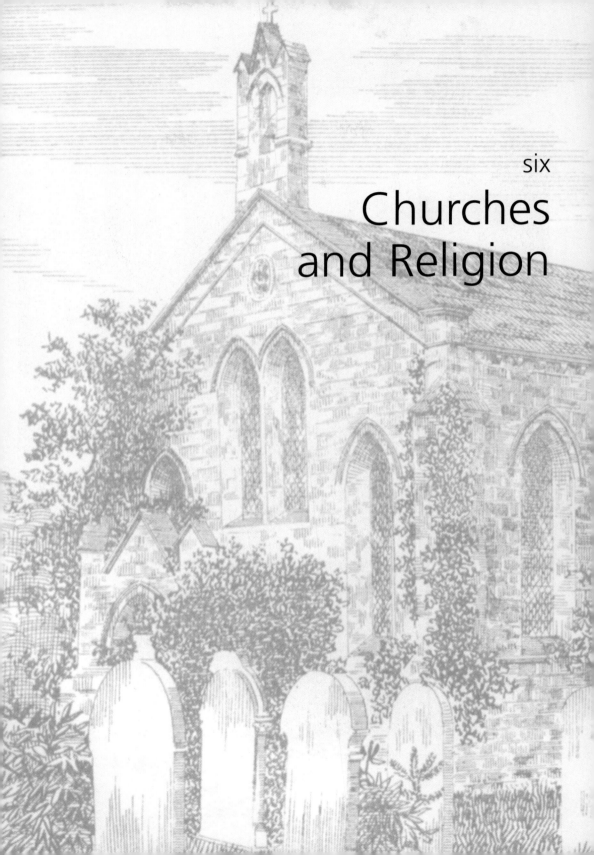

six

Churches
and Religion

Above left: An early picture of the 1662 stone font and its font cover in Rothwell parish church. It was restored in 1902 at the request of Revd Pierson. You can clearly see the stack of Saxon stones and a spare panel on the wall to the left of the font.

Above right: A postcard posted in January 1905, showing the gates to Oulton parish church, built in 1827.

An early photograph of Lofthouse parish church, built in 1839–40.

The original south porch of Rothwell parish church was built in the seventeenth century, but by 1949 was in poor condition. A new porch was built and dedicated to the memory of Revd Francis Gabriel Tallants who had been vicar at Rothwell from 1942 to 1949.

A floodlit view of Rothwell parish church taken in 1931.

We know that this image of Strainer's stonemasons' yard was taken before 1904 because there are no tram wires. The extensive repairs made to the church tower by Harry Stainer in 1877 can be seen.

This rare photograph of Rothwell parish church was taken between 1877 and 1889. Note that there is no lychgate or path leading to the church's south porch.

Flood waters extend to the wall of Rothwell parish church in this photograph, taken in the 1970s.

A view of RUDC's cemetery at the top of Styebank Lane, taken in 1931. Note Girlings' Concrete Works in the centre and the new John O' Gaunts' council estate on the right.

A picturesque view of Rothwell manor house and parish church. The manor house was built by Roger Hopton in 1487 and demolished in 1977. The first mention of a church here in the records of Nostell Priory was in 1130.

The vicarage at Woodlesford is still standing today.

The Oulton Parsonage at the bottom of Leeds Road still stands today.

This is an early view of St Mary's Roman Catholic church, built in the 1930s on what was then the junction of Styebank Lane and Woodlesford Lane.

Rothwell Baptist church on the junction of Wood lane and High Road.

Looking towards Rothwell parish church over the millpond and the pastures of Rothwell in the 1940s.

This old fireplace was part of the old Rothwell vicarage or glebe house, which was built in the fifteenth or sixteenth century. In 1818, the glebe house was deemed to be unfit for residence and records show that in 1834 it no longer existed. The Ripon Diocesan Registry of 1859 refers to a freehold land now used as a garden in Rothwell known, as The Vicarage Garth; the only visible part remaining was this fireplace.

This picture was taken in the 1930s at Rothwell Church of England School then situated on Commercial Street in the centre of Rothwell.

A gathering of the Rothwell Temperance Society. The organ appears to have been taken out of the chapel just for the photograph.

This photograph of Oulton parish church choir was taken in 1914.

This stone is believed to be of Saxon origin and was built into the wall of Rothwell parish church.

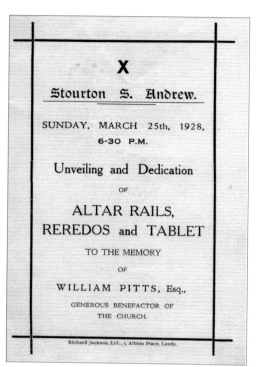

X

Stourton S. Andrew.

SUNDAY, MARCH 25th, 1928,
6-30 P.M.

Unveiling and Dedication

OF

**ALTAR RAILS,
REREDOS and TABLET**

TO THE MEMORY

OF

WILLIAM PITTS, Esq.,

GENEROUS BENEFACTOR OF
THE CHURCH.

Richard Jackson, Ltd., 5, Albion Place, Leeds.

A brochure commemorating the unveiling and dedication of the new Altar Rails, Reredos and Tablet at Stourton St Andrews in 1928.

This picture shows Rothwell parish church prior to the graveyard extension.

A lithograph of Lofthouse church by John Hall of Wakefield produced in 1885.

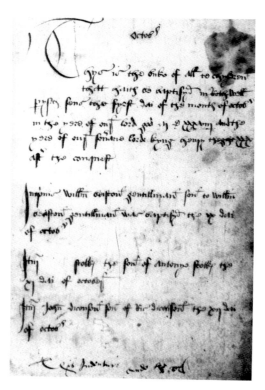

The first entry in the Rothwell parish register
of 1538.

seven

Miscellaneous

The sterrid (or steroid) well on Rothwell pastures close to the old site of Rothwell Manor.

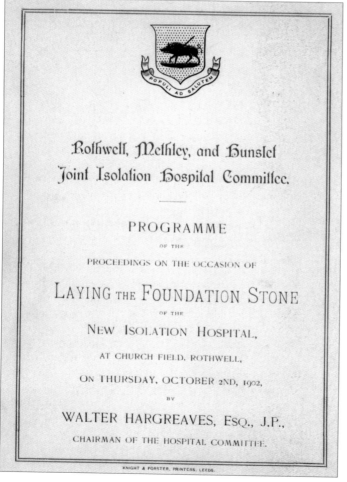

Rothwell, Methley, and Bunslet Joint Isolation Hospital Committee.

PROGRAMME

OF THE

PROCEEDINGS ON THE OCCASION OF

LAYING THE FOUNDATION STONE

OF THE

NEW ISOLATION HOSPITAL,

AT CHURCH FIELD, ROTHWELL,

ON THURSDAY, OCTOBER 2ND, 1902,

BY

WALTER HARGREAVES, ESQ., J.P.,

CHAIRMAN OF THE HOSPITAL COMMITTEE.

KNIGHT & FORSTER, PRINTERS, LEEDS.

This brochure celebrates the laying of the foundation stone of Rothwell Isolation Hospital in 1902.

Opposite above: A Rothwell greeting picture postcard.

Greetings From ROTHWELL

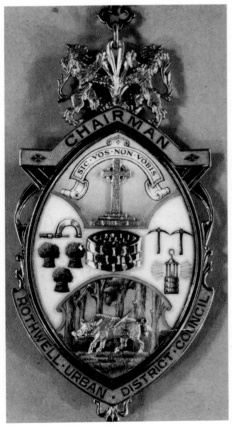

Left: The RUDC Chairman's Chain of Office was presented by Cllr W.E. Moorhouse in February 1938 to commemorate the amalgamation of the Rothwell Urban, Methley Urban and Hunslet Rural Districts. The chain consists of thirty-two gold links with a medallion in gold and enamel. Symbolical figures are embossed on the medallion representing the historical events and industries associated with the Rothwell area.

In his *History of Rothwell*, Batty traces the derivation of the name 'Rothwell' from Rood – a cross and well, thus the central feature of the medallion is the cross surmounting the Well – Rothwell. Immediately after the Norman Conquest, Rothwell was included in the Honour of Pontefract, the Lords of which were the de Lacy's; therefore the rampant Lions at the top of the medallion are from the de Lacy coat of arms. The micrometer not only signifies the engineering industry but also perpetuates the memory of William Cascoigne of Thorpe Hall, the inventor of that instrument.

Coal mining is represented by the pit lamp, stone quarrying by the picks and agriculture by the wheat sheafs. At the base of the medallion is the representation of the last wild boar, reputed to have been killed in the forest of Rothwell Haigh Styebank by John of Gaunt, Duke of Lancaster.

The motto *Sic vos non vobis* may be freely translated as 'Thus by you but not for you', or 'This you do, but not for yourselves.'

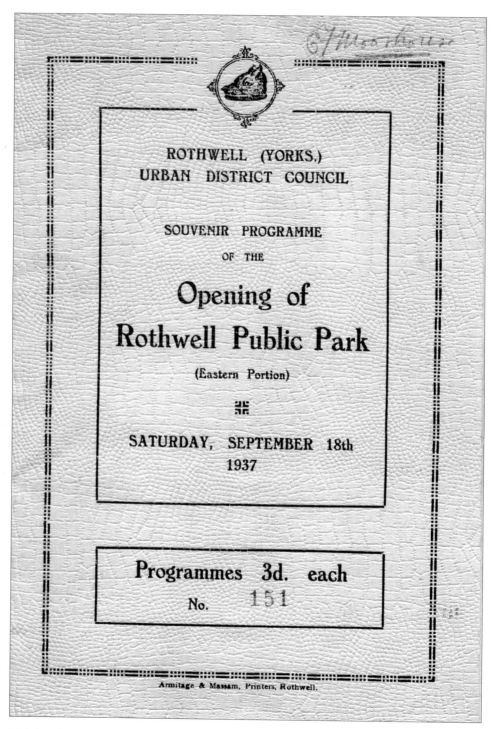

ROTHWELL (YORKS.)
URBAN DISTRICT COUNCIL

SOUVENIR PROGRAMME

OF THE

Opening of

Rothwell Public Park

(Eastern Portion)

SATURDAY, SEPTEMBER 18th
1937

Programmes 3d. each

No. 151

Armitage & Massam, Printers, Rothwell.

This brochure celebrates the opening of Rothwell Public Park in 1937.

This picture was taken for the official brochure commemorating the opening of Rothwell Public Park, which is still to be seen on Park Lane today.

This bandstand has long-since been removed from Rothwell Park. Leeds Road can be seen on the hillside.

This picture was taken outside Springhead House in Rothwell in 1948. June Allen is being crowned queen at the summer festival.

A 1909 multi-postcard showing views of Oulton village.

Drummer George Wright was part of the
Stourton memorial band and his photograph was
taken in around 1917.

This is Stourton Memorial Band, photographed in around 1917. The band was the forerunner to
the Yorkshire Copperworks Band.

Members of staff from Haigh Road School in the late 1940s.

Opposite: Children enjoy a visit from Anita Harris, singer and TV personality, who visited their school in the 1970s and joined them in playing with the craze of the period – the hoola hoop.

Above: Members of kitchen staff at Haigh Road School in the late 1940s. From left to right are: Mrs McCulloch, Jessie Jackson, Gwendolyn Allen, Percy Brown (the school caretaker), Annie Brown (the lunchtime supervisor) and Cissy Arran.

Members of Woodlesford Tennis Club posed for this photograph in 1926.

A photograph of Garnett Higgins who was a Rothwell postman for many years. He is seen here with his delivery bicycle at the junction of Oakwood Drive and Wood Lane.

RUDC gardeners tending the flowerbeds on Leeds Road in Oulton in the 1960s.

The children of Stourton Board School in the early 1900s.

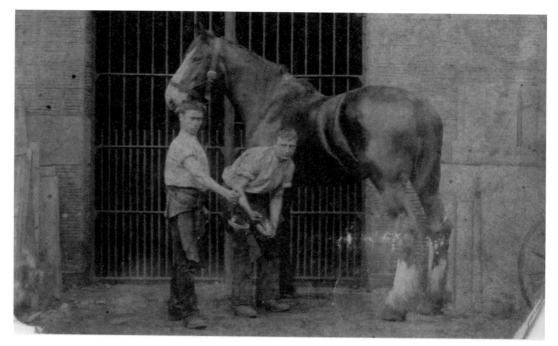

A horse being shoed at Bentleys Brewery in Woodlesford in the early 1960s.

A member of the Ordinance Survey staff pointing out a reference point to his colleague. This photograph, with Fanny Pit in the background, was taken in the 1960s.

A member of the Ordinance Survey staff is here pointing out a reference point at the Stourton Swing Bridge. This photograph was taken in 1960.

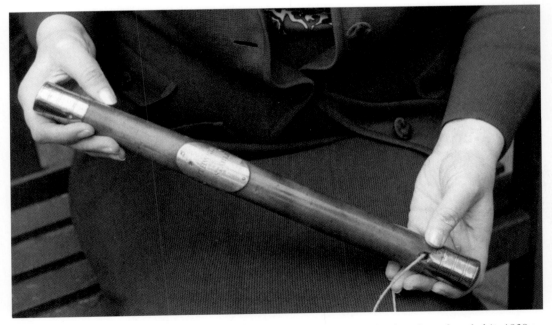

An old Rothwell constables' truncheon used by the area's first paid police force founded in 1839 to police Rothwell, Rothwell Haig and Royds Green. These first constables worked part time and had no uniform but carried truncheons.

Severe flooding at Watergate in Methley in 1960 when the river Calder overflowed its banks after torrential rain.

Oulton Church AFC, in the season 1922/23.

A soup kitchen set up outside the Oulton Institute at Harold Hall during the General Strike of 1926.

Stourton St Andrew's football club in the 1920s.

The opening of the 100th post-war council house in the RDUC area in the 1930s.

Another gathering at the opening ceremony of the 100th post-war council house in the area in the 1930s.

The opening ceremony for Methley Library in February 1948

Cllr E.R. Manley, Chairman of the Housing Committee, presents a book on the National Gallery Collection to the occupier of the 1,000th post-war council house built in the RUDC area. Cllrs Roberts, Buckley and Fowler watch the ceremony in the 1950s.

Above and left: These photographs were taken at Oulton Hall when it was in use as a temporary hospital in the 1940s and '50s. The Grand Hall (above) was used as a dining room. Staff at the hospital are seen here in a Christmas-time photograph (left).

Opposite: A programme for the Masque of Empire day on in 1924. The newspaper of the time reported that there were twenty children in fancy dress on the stage of the Empire Picture house in Rothwell, when a small bit of burning carbon fell from the limelight apparatus. It landed on ten-year old Edith Hurst's dress, which caught fire. Through the quick action of Olive Vinton, who was playing the Queen of Dreams, the fire was put out when she pushed little Edith off the stage and smothered the flames with a rug. Edith's arm was bandaged and a suspension of the play was called. All went back on stage after a short break.

Inside Oulton Hall hospital food store in the 1950s.

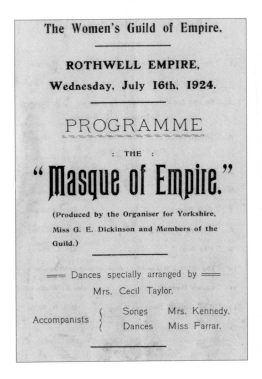

The Women's Guild of Empire.

ROTHWELL EMPIRE,
Wednesday, July 16th, 1924.

PROGRAMME

: THE :

"Masque of Empire."

(Produced by the Organiser for Yorkshire,
Miss G. E. Dickinson and Members of the
Guild.)

=== Dances specially arranged by ===
Mrs. Cecil Taylor.

Accompanists { Songs   Mrs. Kennedy.
              { Dances   Miss Farrar.

Above right: Enid Higgins won first prize at a fancy dress parade when she was dressed as a gypsy woman at the Empire Picture House in Rothwell in 1949.

Mills have occupied this site since the time of the Domesday Book, the last one being demolished in the 1960s. This one was the final one, seen here in the time of Mr Tommy Barrett.

Mrs Fox on baking day at her home on Holmsley Lane in Woodlesford.

A 1920's view of the John O' Gaunt public house in Leeds Road.

A picture of the nurses' home at Rothwell Workhouse, which later became St George's Hospital, in around 1910.

Other local titles published by Tempus

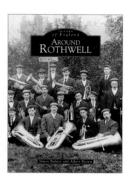

Around Rothwell

SIMON BULMER AND ALBERT BROWN

This selection of over 200 old photographs illustrates the life and times of Rothwell over the last hundred years. Photographs of streets and buildings, industry, people at work and play, schools, churches and special events, contribute to form a nostalgic cavalcade of Rothwell's recent history.
07524 1802 5

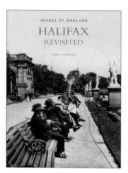

Halifax Revisited

VERA CHAPMAN

This district, characterised by steep slopes and deep valleys, sett-paved streets and nearby moorland and has an industrial past of woollen mills powered by water wheels and steam, is lovingly recreated here to provide a long-lasting record of Halifax as it once was.
07524 3047 5

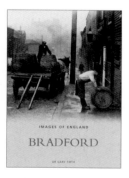

Bradford

GARY FIRTH

This selection of more than 200 images is an attempt to tap into the Bradford once referred to by J.B. Priestley as 'a vast series of pictures, in time and space'. Buildings and streets long since gone and images of Bradford people at work are reproduced here and are sure to stir the memory of all those who went about their business in this vibrant manufacturing city.
07524 3019 X

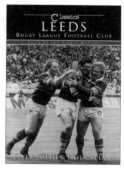

Leeds RLFC Classics

PHIL CAPLAN AND PETER SMITH

Leeds Rugby Club have been in some of the most memorable matches in the sport's history. This book traces Leeds' history from the club's foundation in 1890 through to the 2002 season by detailing fifty of Leeds' most memorable and significant matches.
07524 2740 7

If you are interested in purchasing other books published by Tempus, or in case you have difficulty finding any Tempus books in your local bookshop, you can also place orders directly through our website
www.tempus-publishing.com